CW01083084

Chakr

A Complete Guide to Chakra Healing:
Balance Chakras, Improve your Health and Feel Great

by
Kristine Marie Corr

Table of Contents

Introduction

Welcome and congratulations on taking your first steps towards balancing and healing your chakras. You might have heard people talking about the chakras in terms of how energy flows and works within the body. This may sound like an unusual concept but the truth is that it has been around for generations and continues to influence and benefit people to this very day.

The chakras have long been seen as the most important centers of energy and power in the human body. When the chakras are fully functional, the body can stay healthy and at peace. Naturally, there are many outside forces that can hurt our bodies and keep the chakras from being open. The chakras must be open and flowing if the body and mind are to be healthy. As you will learn in this guide, the chakras are critical to the energy and wellbeing you feel in daily life. They will directly influence many areas relating to your mind and body alike.

This guide will help you to understand what the seven chakras are and how they can help improve your body and your life in general. As you will find out, each individual chakra covers different parts of the body and various emotional and physical aspects of your life. You will learn how to identify the key signs of blocked chakras while also learning about how you can restore their functions. These include many routines that are easy to incorporate into your daily life.

You will also learn about some great habits and exercises that can help energize your body and influence how the chakras form. You will even learn about how to heal the chakras through meditation. The exercises you are about to embark on are very and have the potential to bring great benefits to your life. The chakras are indeed very important to your life and must be treated carefully.

What Are the Chakras?

To understand what the chakras are, we have to look into what the subtle body is. The subtle body is essentially the non physical part of every human being. The **subtle body** can also be defined as the energy that flows in and around the human body. The chakras can be seen as the energy organs of your subtle body. The seven chakras can be looked at as the key points of energy in your body that can influence your mental and emotional state.

Chakra is the Sanskrit word for "wheel" as it refers to the energy that the body can experience. A chakra is visualized as a wheel where the physical world and one's consciousness meet. The energy generated by the wheel is called *Prana*. When the chakras are open, the body will experience energy and well-being.

The chakras have been used in the world of meditation and Ayurvedic medicine for generations. The concept has been around since at least 500 BC as they appear in the Vedas, an ancient Hindu text from India. Each chakra consists of not only the key organs and nerves in your body but also your states of being. There are seven of them and they are aligned along the spinal column moving from the top to the bottom.

The seven chakras work like a network. They are consistently renewing energy in the body. The way they do this is by receiving energy from the food you eat, the amount of exercise you do, your environment, your mental state, and many more important influences. The concept is that each chakra entails a cross between how well your body functions and how your mind can respond. By having a healthy series of chakras that all work well enough and have enough energy, your mind and body will be at ease.

The chakras must be open so that they can allow energy to run through the body. A blockage can be dangerous and difficult to manage. It can cause a chakra to stop functioning as well as it should. It can also cause the other chakras to become stressed out over time. This, in turn, can cause your body to become weak if not treated properly enough. Here is a look at the seven individual chakras. These are organized from the bottom part of your spinal column to the top. The first three relate to matter while the last three are about the spirit.

Muladhara – The Root

The word Muladhara is taken from the Sanskrit work mula, which means "root or base," and adhara, which means support. Located at the base of the spine around the anus and is associated with the color red, which represents vitality. Other colors linked to this chakra are black, brown and silvery grey, which are colors of the soil and earth.

The Muladhara chakra helps you to stay balanced, committed to your work and energetic. It also helps you to digest foods properly. This influences your digestive functions, your bones, teeth, and your sexual health. It also affects your ambition and the drive to move forward in your life.

As this is open, you will begin to feel safe about yourself. You will not fear anything that comes about in your life. This chakra is seen as the foundation as it is known to be the foundation of all the other chakras. It is important to make sure the root chakra is powerful before trying to open and heal the other chakras.

Incense used: Cedar Wood

Crystals and Stones: Garnet, agate, ruby, jasper, bloodstone, and hematite.

Svadhishthana – The Sacral

The word *svadhishthana* is taken from the Sanskrit word *Svad*, which means "one's own," and the word *Adhisthana* that means "residence." This chakra is situated at the base part of the pubis and is linked to the color orange, which represents happiness, creativity, attraction, and success. It affects emotions such as desire, pleasure, and sexuality.

This sacral chakra gives us the ability to feel compassion, have balanced emotions, and be intimate with others. You will feel as though you belong in the world when this chakra is open. The *Svadhishthana* will affect the body's liver, kidneys, spleen and autoimmune system. It influences your emotional identity, how you can manage your personal relationships and how creative you may be. This can particularly influence how creative you are. This chakra will help you to control your creative functions.

Incense used: Gardenia, orris root, and damiana.

Crystals and Stones: Citrine, gold topaz, amber, and moonstone.

Manipura – The Solar Plexus

The word *manipura* is taken from the Sanskrit word *Mani* which means "brilliant or jewel," and the word *Pura* which means "house or city." The Manipura chakra is located between the navel and sternum and is linked with the color yellow, which represents intellectual thinking. When this chakra is balanced, you will exude feelings of confidence, intelligence, energy, and a desire to be productive. You will feel more energetic when this chakra is under control.

In the ancient texts, this chakra sends prana to all areas of the human body. This chakra governs the upper abdomen, your liver, and the stomach. When this chakra is healthy you will experience good physical energy and good digestion. It influences how well you are able to belong in any situation you enter into. It also influences your stamina, your sense of thought and your willingness to move forward.

Incense used: Cinnamon, marigold, carnation.

Crystals and Stones: Gold topaz, amber, gold calcite, and tiger eye.

Anahata – The Heart

The word **Anahata** translated into Sanskrit means "one who dwells within the heart." The Anahata chakra is located in the chest and is linked to the color green, which represents unconditional love. This chakra connects the matter and the spirit together. When the chakra is open, you will feel a sense of the interconnectedness, a feeling of being complete and compassionate. It is this chakra that is responsible for emotions such as hope, trust, forgiveness, empathy, and love.

When the Anahata chakra is healthy you will learn to listen to the voice of your higher self and avoid the wants of the lower self. The Anahata chakra governs the heart and blood, the lungs and the arms. It also affects your feelings of social identity, how you can trust people and how compassionate you are to them. The best way to think of the Anahata chakra is that it is the chakra directly linked to your heart. It focuses on feelings of love and connection with other people and it allows us to trust life.

Incense used: Jasmine, lavender, orris root, and marjoram.

Crystals and Stones: Green jade, emerald, ruby, rose quartz, and malachite.

We will now head into the spiritual chakras below....

Vishuddha – The Throat

The word Vishuddha is taken from the Sanskrit word Shuddhi, which means "purification." The Vishuddha chakra is located in the throat and linked to the color blue, which represents loyalty, confidence, truth, and trust. This chakra influences how you are able to communicate and how you can do this with only the truth in mind.

This chakra is responsible for learning, creativity, communication, and truthfulness. As this chakra open you will be very creative and constructive. You will also be willing to listen to other people's point of view. The Vishuddha governs the throat and parts of the head. It deals with not only communication but also how you are able to take responsibility for the things that you do in your life.

When the Vishuddha is open, you will be able to express yourself well and with confidence. You will be truthful and honest with everyone around you. Physically this chakra influences the throat, teeth, thyroid, and mouth.

Incense used: Frankincense and benzoin.

Crystals and Stones: Blue sapphire, blue topaz, kyanite, turquoise, and aquamarine.

Ajna – The Third Eye

The word Ajna in Sanskrit means "command." The actual translation is "monitoring center." The Ajna chakra is at the centre of the forehead between your eyebrows and is linked to the color indigo that is associated with wisdom, self control, and spiritual awareness. It is considered to be the third eye, the symbolic part of the body that lets you see and know all.

This is what influences the intuition that one may have. When the Ajna is open, it allows you to listen to your intuition whether it entails suggestions or warnings. When it is balanced, it will help you to think and focus on ideas. The third eye is all about staying open and being more observant. This part relates heavily to self-knowledge and wisdom. The chakra helps you to visualize what you want to do with your life. It particularly influences your neurological system and the eyes, ears and other key facial organs.

When the third eye is balanced there is possibility of psychic powers emerging. It is very important to keep the third eye open as it ensures that you won't be stuck thinking about things that you are not comfortable with. You need to pay attention to the warnings that are generated by your third eye.

Incense used: Anise, mugwort, sandalwood, and saffron.

Crystals and Stones: Sodalite, quartz crystal, sapphire, and fluorite.

Sahasrara – The Crown

The word *sahasrara* in Sanskrit means "thousand petal lotus," showing how this chakra has immense potential. It is the last chakra of the seven. It is right on the top of the head and is linked to the color white or violet. When balanced, you will feel as though you are one with the universe. You will feel intelligent and open-minded while having a much easier time with learning new things.

This directly influences brain functions and your emotional thoughts. It can bring about self realization, divine love, and selflessness. As this chakra open, you will feel an amazing feeling of peace. You will also feel as though you are in tune with the things that inspire you the most. All seven of these chakras are critical to your emotional and mental health. You have to make sure you allow the chakras to stay open if you are looking to be healthy and at peace in your life.

Each individual chakra will work separately but at the same time, they all have to be healthy together. Anything that is unhealthy can cause one chakra to stop functioning. This, in turn, can weaken other chakras in some cases. By being active and focusing on healthy and strong exercises, it will be easier for you to keep your prana and energy high. So now we are going to look at the signs and symptoms of blocked chakras.

Incense used: Gotu Kola, and Lotus

Crystals and Stones: White topaz, White Calcite, Amethyst

Signs You Have Blocked Chakras

Just as the chakras contribute to our greater health, if the wheels of energy are not open and working properly, they can contribute to our disease or dis-ease. The imbalances in chakras have an impact on our lives with physical, emotional, and spiritual ramifications.

The negative influence of an imbalanced chakra can prove mild or intense, depending upon the degree of the blockage and how long a person has endured the energy block. In fact, sometimes a blocked chakra can grow worse over the course of time, and other times, the individual adjusts to the influences of the imbalanced chakra energies. Further, Chakras can be over or under stimulated as well, and as such, the symptoms of a malfunctioning chakra will be the same but diminished in comparison to a fully blocked energy vortex.

Below, you will find a list of chakras and information on how energies present in each if there is an issue with the energy vortex, whether it is a partial or full blockage. You very well may find that if you have one chakra that is blocked, you will have more than one blocked. The energy that travels through one chakra influences the other chakras in the energy chain. The restoration of chakra energies so that they are once again in balance is possible and is something we will explore further in the "Healing the Chakras" section of this book.

Imbalances of the Root Chakra

When your root chakra is healthy and allowing the proper flow of prana, you feel a deeply rooted connection to Earth and all life. Often, you will experience the sensations of being sturdy, steadfast, true, and grounded. Your connection to the universe will make you recognize your role in the larger tapestry of life as you simultaneously develop a deep sense of security and support. However, what happens when this vortex of energy is diminished or completely blocked?

Diminished energy flow from this chakra can create physical issues with the parts of the body ruled by this energy vortex. Blocks can lead to issues with the skeletal system and bladder. With the Root Chakra being near the seat of the spine, it should be of little surprise that any imbalances of the chakra would also appear in connection to this area of the body. Indeed, blockages in the flow of root chakra energy can have negative physical effects on the male genitalia, prostate glands, immunological functioning, coccyx bone, rectum, feet, ankles, legs, and knees. Leg cramps, water retention in the legs, venous insufficiency, and varicose veins are also included in the list of physical ailments associated with a blockage in this energy wheel. Finally, this chakra rules the adrenal glands.

With the root chakra's energies diminished, you may feel as if you are having considerable difficulty getting out of an emotional rut or progressing in your life toward goals you have set. The root chakra is one where you will feel naturally grounded, at ease, and relaxed, and your footing is sure, but an imbalance of this chakra can literally "uproot" that secure sense.

When the root chakra is out of balance, you are more likely to endure conditions like constipation, anemia, and bulimia, other eating disorders, sciatica, pain in one or both knees, and degenerative forms of arthritis or bone disease.

The imbalances in chakra energies have an effect on your emotions as well and the obstruction will present itself as negative feelings and conditions related to food, shelter, and the "bare bone" necessities of life. Think of how a root nourishes a plant and then think of the "root" chakra as an energy wheel allowing you to draw energies up and through it to the other chakras. The Root Chakra is one that serves as a nourishing chakra: One that needs to be in good health so the chakras above it can thrive. Think of this energy wheel as a "root" system drawing up nourishment from the Earth Mother below it. Thus, the energy system is only as healthy as the root system that nourishes it. The root chakra is the energy vortex that keeps us connected to that which sustains us.

Imbalances of the Sacral Chakra

The types of imbalances that occur to the physical body when the sacral chakra is not functioning properly include issues with the female reproductive organs and kidneys. The individual may also develop issues with the lower back, hips, and the pelvic region. Issues with the menstrual cycle, gynecological conditions, and urinary tract infections are associated with blocks in this energy wheel.
When this chakra is out of balance there are issues related to relationships and commitments. You may suddenly find you have considerable difficulty when you want to express yourself on an emotional level. This chakra rules over your playful and pleasure energies and, therefore, has an impact on the joy (or lack thereof) that you feel in relation to sex and creativity. Since this chakra rules the pleasure centers, it is also associated with additions, betrays, and potential impotence.

When the Sacral Chakra is obstructed, you may feel physically or emotionally tired and/or overwhelmed. Lethargy, a lack of motivation, and, sometimes, lackadaisical behavior are the result of blocks in this chakra's energy.

A balanced Sacral Chakra allows for you to move forward in life with confidence while taking well-considered risks, and allows us to embrace adventure. This Chakra connects us to the Divine and the universe through creativity, and it is associated without outgoing, highly sexual, and passionate nature while simultaneously ruling over our deep sense of commitments when in a relationship with another.

Imbalances of the Solar Plexus Chakra

When the Solar Plexus is in a healthy energetic state, we are both compassionate and respectful with ourselves. This chakra allows us to feel confidence, to assert ourselves and to confidently take control of the wheel of our lives. If we through this chakra out of balance we may suddenly experience issues with the gastrointestinal system, colon, gallbladder, pancreas, and liver. Along the same lines, we might experience a metabolic disorder like diabetes onset. Issues with the gut lead to skin conditions including dermatitis, acne, and eczema, among other skin conditions. Chronic fatigue, hypertension, and digestive dis-eases of all kinds come with the imbalance of the Solar Plexus. This chakra can lead to issues with mood regulation as well since the gut and mind are so intricately connected.

When the imbalance of this chakra influences how you are feeling, you may feel as if your self-esteem has bottomed out or that you have been stripped of your personal power. You may find that it is easier to engage in negative self-talk because your inner critic is alive and well as it tears you down psychologically. The imbalance of the energies of this chakra also come with issues related to being critical of the self and others.

Blockages in this energy wheel have been known to leave the individual stressed out, fatigued, mentally drained, exhausted, and feeling run down or on the edge of illness. The solar plexus chakra out of balance can lead to ambiguous intuitive sensations that one has difficulty discerning, and this can cause anxiety or anxious feelings in the sufferer.

Imbalances of the Heart Chakra

In its healthy state, the Heart Chakra lets us feel love, compassion, gratitude, joy, and give forgiveness. If your heart chakra is imbalanced, you will experience a number of physical ailments in the upper torso, including the breasts, lungs, and heart. Some symptoms include issues related to the asthmatic conditions, lymphatic system, wrists, shoulders, and upper back region. The heart chakra can influence how the immune system functions as well as the health of the Thymus Gland in the body. The Thymus Gland produces T-cells and plays a vital role in the correct functioning of the body's natural immunological functioning. In terms of an emotional presentation, an imbalanced Heart Chakra can have someone feeling lonely, bitter, furious, abandoned, jealous, or suffocated emotionally.

The heart chakra's energies help you connect with the world on a compassionate and empathic level. If obstructed, you may find it difficult to reach out to others, and you might experience a cold sense of detachment from loved ones or the world in general. The blockages of the heart chakra can be felt most intensely on an emotional level as we can lose our sense of compassion, love, and that, which is beautiful. An obstructed heart chakra is, therefore, akin to a "broken heart" with the onset of a loss of hope, faith, passion, trust, and the birth of an apathetic, distrusting, aloof nature. On a physical level, a broken heart can do much damage: One can seemingly age far more rapidly with blocked chakra energies.

Imbalances of the Throat Chakra

A healthy Throat Chakra state is identified by one's ability to communicate well, express one's self, and to make it known to others that you are an excellent, compassionate, and experienced listener. When in imbalance presents itself you may suddenly experience a loss for the right words, or the inability to talk to someone beyond a superficial level. On a metaphysical level, the Throat Chakra relates to one's ability to create, to experience and express a Divine connection, and to manifest one's desires (considering here the power behind the spoken words "I am.")

If you experience something extremely traumatic, this can close off the throat chakra. It, therefore, produce issues with self-expression. Edginess, crankiness, fear, anxiety, nervousness, Attention Deficit Disorder, Attention Deficit Hyperactivity Disorder, and the absence of skills that would otherwise allow you to serve as a guide or mentor for another: These issues stem from the energy blocks in the Throat Chakra.

When your Throat Chakra is out of balance, you may experience issues related to your neck shoulders, hands, and arms, but you may experience problems in the facial region as well. For example, imbalances can produce issues with the tongue, lips, cheek, or chin, as well as ulcers, ear infections, Temporomandibular Joint Disorder "TMJ," laryngitis, sore throats, tonsillitis, and thyroid and esophageal issues. The emotional presentation of such an imbalance appears as a lack of willpower, the sense of being out of control or the literal act of having in control, and the fear of having no choice in a matter.

Additional imbalance indications include issues with spoken or written forms of communication.
An over-stimulated Throat Chakra may present in a person as an excessively loud, grating or coarse voice and the desire to manipulate the will of others by imposing one's perspective on them. An under-stimulated chakra can result in someone who engages in self-neglect or it may cause a person to put the needs of others before the needs of the self. A blocked throat chakra can also result in a person feeling victimized, guilty, or it can result in dishonest behavior, particularly speech.

Physically, this chakra might present as infections of the throat, mouth, tonsils, and headaches caused by neck tension. Thyroid conditions and the secondary symptoms of an overactive/underactive thyroid, insomnia, allergic responses, and skin conditions also result from a blocked Throat chakra. A block of this chakra affects one's ability for self-expression: Ask the question: What's under your skin? – This is how skin conditions manifest as a result from this chakra being blocked improperly stimulated.

Imbalances in the Third Eye Chakra

With the third eye, you can see your life and all there is from an elevated or even an illuminated standpoint. When the chakra is working properly, you will feel clear, alert, intensely focused and your concentration will prove considerable. As this chakra operates correctly, you are open to insight, wisdom, and deep knowing thereby allowing an easier assessment of what is true and what is not.

Imbalances in this particular chakra can cause an array of physical ailments including hormonal imbalances, loss of hearing, seizures, eye fatigue or blurry vision, sinusitis and issues with allergies, and headaches as well as migraines.

When it comes to the emotional level, the Third Eye chakra's imbalance can result in a lack of concentration that leads to daydreaming, anxiety, an overused imagination, excessive or erroneous self-reflection, rapid and irregular shifts in moods, and volatile behavior.

The Third Eye rules the head, temple, forehead and the endocrine and lymphatic systems. The Pineal Gland, a gland in the center of the brain, is ruled by the Third Eye Chakra. René Descartes called the pineal gland "the principal seat of the soul." This gland is responsible for generating melatonin, which is a natural substance affecting one's sleep patterns. An imbalanced chakra may result in an interruption or change in sleep patterns, either excessive sleep or insomnia. This Chakra is associated with a high level of ethereal energy and one's innate psychic talents; thus, a block in this chakra may inhibit one's ability to tap into one's intuitive responses or gut response.

Imbalances of the Crown Chakra

As the Root Chakra allows us to remain grounded and to make a connection with the Earth Mother, the Crown Chakra is our Sky Father or Divine Connection, joining us with the Universe. The Crown Chakra is one that, when healthy, allows us to enjoy each moment of life, to live "in this very moment," and to be aware of each passing instant. Mindful living is the result of a healthy Crown Chakra. The physical ailments one develops when this chakra is out of balance include an excessive sensitivity to environmental stimuli, sounds, or light. Light migraines and seeing of auras (visual aberrations) can also result.

The improper working of this chakra can have an impact on one's ability to learn and to assimilate new knowledge with existing understandings. Since this Chakra rules the upper crown and head region, an imbalance can result in depression and other mood aberrations. Emotionally, the crown chakra's improper workings can result in close-minded thinking, religious/ spiritual intolerance, a lack of acceptance, an inability to forgive, and the birth of fear and prejudice.

An improperly stimulated crown chakra results in a sense of isolation or intentional separation from others. The blocked crown chakra can result in a time of cocooning, where the individual spends a great deal of time struggling with the sense of being alone and the loneliness that comes with such a state. One's own thoughts will justify one's desire for isolation, but the enforced isolation is a vicious cycle resulting in feelings of confusion, alienation, abandonment, and despair.

Imbalances in the crown chakra can result in physical ailments including issues with bones, paralysis, and Multiple Sclerosis. A loss of one's spiritual connection is also possible. Nervous system conditions, mood disorders, depression, and anxiety are symptoms of a blocked chakra energy vortex as well. This Chakra rules the head and therefore rules the entire body: Thus, an imbalance in its energies can result in systemic conditions and issues with autoimmunity.

The Causes of Blockages and Healing Chakra Imbalances

There are different factors that have role in the unwanted development of chakra blockages. Once you know what these factors are you can take some preventative action and try to avoid them – this will help to reduce or even eliminate some of the blockages you might have otherwise developed in the future. With an understanding about the suspected causes of energy blocks in the chakras, you can also begin to identify some of the potential methods for healing the imbalances that occur.

An imbalanced chakra can be over stimulated, under stimulated or completely blocked. The different causes of energy blocks can be encountered in differing degrees of intensity, so the amount of energy effected or how the chakra is influenced differs from one person to another. A person's tolerance of external stimuli also plays a role in the level or degree of a developed imbalance. With each chakra, as we covered earlier, there are different issues and dis-eases that arise.

Positive Habits and How They Influence The Chakras

The best thing that you can do in order to keep the chakras flowing and functional is to make a few important changes in your life. The changes that you can make are essential as they relate heavily to allowing your body and mind to stay focused and healthy.

Naturally, you might think that taking medications or medicines to help you out with recovering from the signs and symptoms of blocked chakras is a good idea. While medicines can be helpful for many things, in some cases you will end up suffering from the same problem, later on, thus forcing you to take even more medicine to resolve the issue. You might have gotten rid of that headache earlier in the day but it will be back later on and you have to interrupt your day to take some medicine to resolve it.

You will have less of a need – or maybe even no need – to be dependent on such things if you can get your chakras to function properly. As you engage in a series of healthy habits, it will be easier for the chakras to be restored and controlled in a proper fashion.

Dietary Habits

The foods that we eat on a daily basis can directly influence our lives and our prana. There's a reason why people say that you are what you eat.

By sticking with healthier and easier to follow dietary habits, it will be easier for the body to keep the chakras functioning properly. There are many great aspects of your diet that can work to help you keep your body flowing with energy.

Keeping You Grounded

When the Muladhara chakra is blocked this may cause you to not feel grounded and concentrated. You should focus on root vegetables to improve the Muladhara. Root vegetables like carrots, potatoes and beets are always worthwhile. Healthy proteins like eggs, meat, quinoa and soy can help too.

You must be grounded if you want to feel happier in your life. When you are grounded you are in tune with the world and can face challenged with a cool and calm attitude. You must be grounded to stay healthy and less likely to be fearful. Meditation can help you feel grounded and I go into more detail about how you can incorporate mediation it into your daily life in my free ebook that you find out about at the end of this book.

Enhance Your Intuition With Antioxidants

Your intuition will work better if you are focused and your chakras are open. You have to enhance the power of the chakras to allow your intuition to operate properly so you will have a clearer mind. Antioxidants are especially important for your body and the energy that flows through it.

Your body can become filled with free radicals throughout the day. These oxygen particles can get in the way of your body and keep cellular functions from being normal. It will be easier for your body to wear out and develop fatigue if you have too many free radicals.

Antioxidants are used to help eliminate those free radicals. These components bind to those oxygen particles with ease. The best part is that you can get plenty of foods in your diet to help you out with getting the antioxidants that you demand. To start, you will require plenty of antioxidant-rich fruits to help you keep your chakras open. These include blueberries, strawberries, and pomegranates among other items. The acai berry can also be ideal to consider.

Having more greens in your diet can help just as well. Whether it is from spinach, lettuce or kale among other items, you can certainly benefit from having greens that will keep your body healthy and comfortable. This is thanks to the antioxidants that you will get from these foods as well as digestive enzymes to help break down those foods.

By having enough antioxidants, you can improve your immunity levels and digestive functions while also having more energy. As you develop more energy, your mind will begin to clear up. The chakras can all start to work properly.

Best of all, this energy boost can come without the use of caffeine. This is ideal as caffeine can make people jittery at times and can cause the chakras to weaken after a period of time due to how they went through more stress than what is necessary.

The Energetic Influences of Others

In some cases, a person's energies can influence your energies when you encounter the individual. This is particularly true if you are an empath and your ability to pick up on other people's energy and emotional vibrations are intensified. If you have ever encountered someone and had "some bad vibes" about a person, or some unexplained negative feelings, then you know the feeling of undesirable mingled energies. If you have ever been somewhere in a good mood and suddenly, without explanation your mood shifts rapidly (matching that of someone else in a poor mood nearby), then you know what is like to have another person's energies mingle with yours and cause a change in your personal vibration.

Just as there are those who, willingly or unwillingly mingle their negative energy with your own, there are those who like to take away your personal energy – these psychic vampires like to drain you of the energy in your psychic body, and this can lead to an under active or blocked chakra in more than one area.

External Triggers of Chakra Blocks

Emotions play a serious role in the functioning of your chakras. If, for example, you go through a stressful or traumatic event, or if you endure some significant emotional upset, it will likely leave its mark in the functioning of the chakra system. Stress can wreak havoc on chakra functioning, just as it does the physical and mental bodies. Negative emotions, phobias, anxiety, loss, conflict, arguments, depression, negative or low moods – all can either be evidence of malfunctioning charka or can contribute to the actual malfunction. In an effort to protect the energetic body, the chakra might become blocked off completely and it may close – this is part of the natural defense system – a built in coping mechanism. If left untreated, this condition can lead to discomfort and disease.

When one chakra is not working properly, eventually other chakras will also start to malfunction. Some chakras may slow down while others become over-active. The method for fixing all malfunctioning chakras is to work on the closed or block chakras so that they reopen and function correctly. Once these chakras begin working correctly, those charkas that were over-active and attempting to compensate will no longer need to do so.

Chakra Block – A General Healing Technique

In the event you encounter people who seem to "rub you the wrong way," or affect your personal energies, it is time to block your chakras so that their energies will not have sway over yours. It is advised that you turn away from the source of negativity as quickly as possible: Politely pull back your personal energies and, as you do so, cross both of your arms over the gut area or solar plexus chakra. Doing this action helps to disturb the energy flow and slow down the amount of negative energy you are absorbing from another. In regard to psychic vampires who feed on the energies of another, you must learn to recognize these individuals for what they are – only then can you appropriately deal with their parasitic, draining behaviors.

The psychic vampire will feed directly off your natural life force energy, the prana flowing through each chakra. The symptoms that often accompany this action include depression, mood swings, and fatigue. If you are noting such symptoms and you suspect a vampire is responsible, envision yourself surrounded by a protective bubble of pure white light. Let the light force out all negative and block the entrance of external energies into the chakras.

Aromatherapy

Aromatherapy involves the use of essential oils for the purposes of healing and relaxation: The process is used to support natural healing modalities. There are specific scents associated with each chakra, and in using each scent you can help in restoring the chakra to normal function. It may take several aromatherapy sessions for you to achieve maximum effect. While some people like to use the oils directly, others like to burn the oils in an oil burner or to use them in an oil diffuser. Some oils can be added to bath water to induce relaxation and to help in restoring the energy system to full health. Below is a list of the appropriate oils you can use with each chakra.

Please note: If you have never used aromatherapy before, take the appropriate cautions and speak with a professional aromatherapist for more in depth advice. There are some dermal safety precautions you might want to consider before using oils, and you will want to ensure you buy only best quality oils for your personal use. For more information on aromatherapy and the use of essential oils, visit: The National Assocation of Holistic Aromatherapy.

Chakra	Essential Oil Use for Healing
Root: To be applied to the base of one's spine.	Patchouli – preferred for its "earthy" scent, which connects it to mother earth, grounding, and the root chakra. Alternative oils include Ginger, Cypress,

	Gingerwood,
Sacral: To be applied just above the belly button.	Sandalwood – preferred as a sensual scent and one that aligns with the energies of the reproductive organs. Alternatives include Clary Sage, Rosewood, and Patchouli.
Solar Plexus: To be applied between the rib cage and the belly button.	Lemon – a citrus scent promoting proper circulatory processes, toning, and respiration. Alternatives include Fennel and Juniper oils.
Heart: To be applied at the heart region.	Pine – Preferred as a stimulating scent. Alternative scents include Ylang Ylang, Rose, and Jasmine.
Throat: To be applied at the throat.	Lavender – Preferred for its relaxing effect. Alternatives include Geranium, Chamomile, and Bergamot.
Third Eye: To be applied in the middle of the forehead.	Frankincense – Preferred for its purifying properties. Alternatives include Cedarwood and Patchouli.
Crown: To be applied at the top of the head.	Myrrh – Preferred for its stimulating properties. Alternatives include Lavender and Frankincense.

Affirmations

Affirmations are short statements of intention that you can use to help in rebalancing your chakras. You can create your own affirmations so that the intention behind each statement is personalized. As you work with each statement of intent, the more you repeat the statement, the more you draw similar energies to you while simultaneously triggering your subconscious to accept what you are saying as true or as a state that is already in existence. There is a number of things you can do with affirmations. First, the option of repeating the statement throughout the day will serve as a continued reminder of your intention. Second, you write the affirmation on a piece of paper and tape the note anywhere you know you will see it. Every time you see it, say it out loud. When meditating, you can think of the affirmation repeatedly. The use of the affirmations in this way will help align the subconscious and conscious, and will trigger the body's natural healing processes.

Each chakra is associated with a phrase that can be integrated into affirmations. The phrases are as follows:

Chakra and Phrase	• Sample Affirmations
Root: "I do," or "I am."	"I am deeply connected to my Earth Mother." "I am well-grounded and balanced." "I do have enough to meet my needs." "I am enough."
Sacral: "I want," or "I feel."	"I want to experience joy in my life." "I want a good and well-controlled relationship with money." "I feel content and satisfied." "I feel creative."
Solar Plexus: "I do," or "I can."	"I do have the power to manifest what I want in my life." "I do feel self confident." "I can manifest my desires." "I can do anything."
Heart: "I love."	"I love myself." "I love my family." "I love my life." "I love the blessings I receive."
Throat: "I express" or "I speak."	"I speak with conviction." "I speak honestly."

	"I express myself eloquently."
	"I express myself with ease."
Third Eye: "I think" or "I know."	*"I know without knowing."*
	"I know that I know nothing."
	"I think clearly."
	"I think with organized thoughts."
Crown: "I understand" or "I am."	*"I am awakened."*
	"I am enlightened."
	"I understand my life's purpose."
	"I understand myself and I show myself compassion."

Herbals

Certain herbs are ideal for dealing with chakra energy imbalances. Just as chakras are centers of energy, plant life carries its own energy vibrations – these vibrations can be used to match or stimulate the vibrations of specific chakras. The vibration frequencies of the specific herbs one chooses helps in restoring the balance of the mind, body, and spirit. When using the herbals you can trigger a chakra into action, because it reopen, or to slow down if it is over stimulated. Herbs can be consumed in an effort to detox the energy centers as well and free them of negative vibrations or energy sources.

The way in which herbs can be used are myriad – they can be consumed in dried form and used for making teas or decoctions, and you can also use herbal remedies in salves, lotions, creams, powders, oils, tinctures, tablets, and capsules. Before using any herbs, discuss it with your doctor and a qualified herbalist to ensure your safety. Pregnant women as well as breast feeding mothers should avoid the use of herbals. If you have a pre-existing health condition, definitely get a doctor's consent before using any herbs. Some herbs can interact with over the counter and prescribed medications and can affect the efficacy of the drugs in question.

Chakra	Recommended Herbals and Application
Root	Ginseng – Preferred for its ability to help you ground. Any reddish root or earthy herb applies. Alternatives include Clover, Ginger Root, Echinacea, Cayenne Pepper, Dong Quai, Damiana, and Yucca.
Sacral	Calendula – Preferred. Herbs that are orange in color or that has a high level of water content applies. Alternatives include Grape Seed and Papaya.
Solar Plexus	Milk Thistle – Preferred. Those herbs that are beneficial to one's liver apply. Alternatives include Parsley, Dandelion, Ginger, Lemon Balm, Yarrow, and Mettle.
Heart	Rose Hips – Preferred. Herbs that are good for dealing with cardiovascular conditions and support apply. Alternatives include Sage, Echinacea, Pine, Hawthorn, and Pine.
Throat	Chamomile – Preferred. Herbs with relaxing agents apply. Alternatives include herbals like Eucalyptus, Thyme, Primrose Oil, Fennel, Hyssops, and Witch Hazel.

Third Eye	Skullcap – Preferred. Stimulating herbs apply. Alternatives include herbals like White Willow Bark, Passionflower, Lobelia, Kava, Bilberry, Vervain, and Valerian.
Crown	Valerian – Preferred . Herbs that enhance the memory and improve cognitive functioning apply. Alternatives include Meadowsweet, Vervain, and Gotu Kola.

Gemstones & Crystals

Just as there are special phrases and herbs associated with each chakra, there are crystals you can use that have similar or matching vibrations for each chakra. These special crystals influence the human aura when they are positioned nearby the body or when they are worn by an individual. Crystals can contribute to one's healing by helping in activating a chakra that is closed, stimulating a slow spinning chakra, or slowing down and over active energy vortex.

Your intentions are coupled with a crystal's energies to determine how the stone will work. Stones are sacred tools that can be cleansed, consecrated, and charged for specific purposes, particularly for energy purification purposes, healing, and for protection from being exposed to negative energies in the future as well. For the most part, there are many crystals that will work with each chakra and the color of the stone often matches up with the color of the chakra in question.

Crystals can be placed directly on the body – you can lie down and put the crystals right on the center of the chakras you are looking to cleanse and balance. The stones are ideal for use during visualization exercises and mediations that will help in healing the chakra system. The stones make wonderful jewelry pieces that can serve as 24 hour protection against negative energies influencing the body, mind, and spirit.

Before the gemstones can be used for healing the chakra system, the stones have to be cleansed and should also be charged. There are myriad means for doing this, but the simplest is to run the stones under some cool water to clean them physically. Put the out and let them sit out in the moonlight for a few nights. Some people prefer sunlight and this is acceptable as well. Allow the planetary bodies to naturally charge the stones for you before you use them. You can also hold them in your hand and charge them for a specific purpose, like balancing a chakra, or slowing the energy wheel down or speeding it up.

Chakra	Recommended Gemstone/Crystal and Usage
Root	Bloodstone – Preferred because it is considered a "Nurturing goddess stone," and one that makes an ideal amulet. The stone helps in increasing one's self confidence. It is a stone that supports growth, renewal, productivity, and health. Alternatives include Ruby, Red Tiger's Eye, Garnet, Red Obsidian, Smoky Quartz, Pyrite, Red Hematite, Black Tourmaline, and Onyx.
Sacral	Copper preferred for it stimulating properties. Alternative stones include Carnelian, Vanadinite, Tiger's Eye, Tiger Iron, Turquoise, and Fluorite.
Solar Plexus	Citrine preferred for its attracting and stimulating properties. Alternative stones include Gold, Citrine, Amber, Calcite, Yellow Jasper, and Yellow Jade.
Heart	Peridot preferred for its

	soothing vibrations. Alternatives include Malachite, Emerald, Aventurine, Jade, Watermelon Tourmaline, Unakite, Ruby, Rose Quartz, Aventurine, Chrysocolla, and Chrysoprase.
Throat	Blue Agate preferred for its soothing and cooling properties. Alternatives include Sodalite, Angelite, Lapis Lazuli, Sapphire, Amazonite, Topaz, Blue Kyanite, Turquoise, and Blue Calcite.
Third Eye	Quartz for its stimulating and clarifying properties. Alternative stones include Crystal Tanzanite,, Sugilite, Sapphire, Lapis Lazuli, Azurite, and Amethyst.
Crown	Amethyst – Preferred for its color and sobering properties. Alternative stones include Serpentine, Quartz, and Diamond.

Diversity in Healing

Our energy centers must remain in balance if we are to experience the best state of physical, mental, emotional, and spiritual health. However, there are so many things in the world, such as our encounters with others, external stimuli, and traumatic events, which can set our energy vortexes spinning too quickly, too slow, or can stop them from spinning at all. Thankfully, we can restore balance of our chakra system with relative ease and with holistic means. Via meditation, visualization, the use of gems, stones, and affirmations, as well as the use of specific phrases and creative affirmations can help us restore our energy centers to optimal health. A mixed approach to healing is best where you rely on more than one natural healing modality to maximize the health of each energy center and to clear any blockages from your chakra system.

If you would like to read my Free Ebook on how different meditation techniques can help to open the chakras please visit

http://freechakrabook.gr8.com

Printed in Great Britain
by Amazon